The Arabian Desert

CW00866926

Written by Anita Ganeri

Contents

The Arabian Desert	2
Seas of sand	4
Desert weather	12
Plucky plants	18
Animal survival	24
Desert people	34
Riches of the desert	44
Changing desert	50
Glossary	52
Index	53
Arabian Desert quiz	54

Collins

The Arabian Desert

Deserts are dry places where very little rain falls. Sometimes, years go by without any rain at all. By day, deserts may be baking hot but at night, they can be freezing cold. Some are hot in summer but cold in winter. Some deserts are mostly sandy but others are rocky, stony or covered in salt, or a mixture of all of these.

The Arabian Desert in the Middle East is one of the biggest and sandiest deserts in the world. It covers an area of about 2,330,000 square kilometres. The desert covers most of the Arabian **Peninsula**, and lies mostly in the country of Saudi Arabia.

Syria
Israel
Jordan
Iraq
Egypt
Kuwait
Iran
Qatar
U.A.E.
Oman
Red Sea
Saudi Arabia
Sudan
Yemen
Indian Ocean

The Arabian Desert

Did you know?

Deserts cover about a third of the land on Earth. There are deserts in Asia, Africa, North America, South America and Australia. Strictly speaking, Antarctica (shown here) also counts as a desert because it's so dry.

Seas of sand

Large parts of the Arabian Desert are covered in sand. Sand is made up of tiny fragments of rock which have been ground down by water and the wind. The sand in the Arabian Desert is mostly made up of two types of rocks, called quartz and feldspar. Feldspar gives the sand a reddish-orange colour.

The scorching Rub al Khali, one of the most hostile habitats on Earth.

Huge seas of sand cover the desert. In the Arabic language, they are known as *ergs*. The largest erg is the Rub al Khali. It covers around 660,000 square kilometres – about the size of France – and is the biggest sand sea in the world.

Rub al Khali means "Empty Quarter". It gets its name because this part of the desert is so hot, dry and sandy that no one can live there all the time. Apart from the hostile climate, the huge sand dunes make it difficult for people to move around.

red sand in the Arabian Desert

The Rub al Khali is famous for its sand dunes. These are giant, wave-like heaps of sand, piled up by the wind blowing across the ground. In the Rub al Khali, the dunes can reach more than 200 metres in height, as tall as a 50-storey building.

The sand dunes come in different shapes, depending on the speed and direction of the wind. Barchan dunes form when the wind blows steadily from one direction. If there's something in the way, such as a rock or bush, the flow slows down. The sand builds up around the obstacle to make a crescent shape.

barchan dunes

Some dunes form in long, straight lines, **parallel** to the wind. In the Rub al Khali, the lines can be 300 kilometres long. These dunes are called *seif* dunes. Seif is the Arabic word for "sword", and the dunes look like a row of sharp sword blades.

Israel
Jordan
Iraq
Iran
Kuwait
Qatar
Saudi Arabia
U.A.E.
Oman
Yemen

The Arabian Desert
The Rub al-Khali

seif dunes

Sand may be
the most famous feature
of the Arabian Desert, but
there are also high mountains,
rocky **plateaux** and steep cliffs.
The highest mountain is Mount
Al-Nabi Shu'ayb in Yemen which

Iran

U.A.E.

Saudi Arabia

Oman

▲ Yemen

Mount
Al-Nabi Shu'ayb

stands 3,760 metres tall. There are also long lines of
spectacular cliffs, hundreds of kilometres long.

The mountains and cliffs are carved into shape by water
running down their slopes. The water runs in valleys,
called *wadis*. Wadis are
usually dry, but if there's
a sudden fall of
heavy rain, they
quickly fill to
overflowing and
then the water
rushes downhill in
a torrent.

water flowing
through a wadi

Did you know?

Some parts of the desert are covered in huge black patches of **lava**. The lava comes from volcanoes that first erupted millions of years ago. Today, scientists monitor the volcanoes carefully in case they should erupt again.

Other parts of the Arabian Desert are covered in vast, flat plains. Some of the plains are rocky or stony because any sand has been blown away by the wind. The stones were left behind by ancient rivers millions of years ago. The rivers carried huge loads of rock, mud and sand, but dried up long ago.

These stony plains in the Arabian Desert are known as hammada.

This area, the Sabkah Matti, is the largest sabkah in the Arabian Desert.

Near the coast, there are sandy plains that are covered in a salty crust, formed by trapped sea water. The water dried up in the sun, leaving the salt behind. These plains are called *sabkhahs*, and can be very dangerous.

The salt mixes with mud and sand to make a slush, like quicksand, with a hard crust on top. There are many tales of travellers who stepped onto the crust and found themselves sinking into the quicksand. One story tells how a whole herd of goats disappeared!

Desert weather

It's baking hot in the Arabian Desert, especially in the summer when the temperature can reach a scorching 54 degrees centigrade. Winters are cooler, with temperatures sometimes falling below freezing. There are clear skies and plenty of sunshine all through the year.

In January 2015, a snowstorm brought heavy snow to the Arabian Desert. It was the third year running that snow had fallen. The snow stayed long enough for Bedouin shepherds to have the unusual experience of building a snowman.

The desert air can play tricks with your eyes. You might think that you can see water in the distance but it's actually a mirage. This happens when a layer of cold air traps a layer of hot air next to the ground. The layers bend light coming from the sky, making it look like water.

These camels look as if they are walking through water.

Deserts are the driest places on Earth. Most of the Arabian Desert gets less than 100 millimetres of rain a year, and some parts are even drier than that. The rain falls mainly in winter and spring, between November and May.

Occasionally, there are thunderstorms which bring heavy rain. The rain fills the wadis, turning them into raging torrents and causing flash floods. Flash floods can happen with almost no warning and can be very dangerous. They sweep away anything in their path, including large boulders, cars and even people.

a desert valley after a rare fall of rain

Hundreds of thousands of years ago, the Arabian Desert was much wetter and greener than it is today. Scientists have discovered traces of thousands of ancient rivers and lakes. These were home to animals, such as hippopotamuses, water buffalo and elephants, which aren't found in the desert today.

Winter and spring are very windy in the Arabian Desert. Winds blow as fast as 150 kilometres per hour and can last for weeks on end. They can knock down tents and trees, and carve out huge holes or dips in the sand dunes, changing their shape.

As the wind races across the ground, it whips up choking clouds of sand and dust. These storms can last for days. "Brown rollers" are huge storms that may be up to 100 kilometres wide. They look like huge brown clouds of sand and dust, rolling along the ground.

"brown roller" storm travelling over Riyadh, Saudi Arabia

Sometimes, the sand and dust is so thick that it can be difficult to see and breathe. People cover their mouths and noses, or stay indoors. The wind can also pick up many tonnes of sand, then dump it kilometres away.

After a sandstorm, bulldozers are sometimes used to clear the sand from the roads.

Plucky plants

Despite the tough conditions, an amazing number of plants and animals live in the Arabian Desert. They have a wide range of features to help them stay alive.

Plants need water to make their food, and although water is scarce in the desert, many plants manage to survive. A shrubby plant, called abal, grows on the slopes of sand dunes. It has spreading, shallow roots to soak up as much moisture as possible.

Other plants have special stems and leaves for saving and storing water.

To avoid the dry weather, some desert plants lie buried as seeds. They can stay like this for months, or even years. The seeds have a special coating that stops them growing until it rains, when the water washes the coating off. Then the seeds start sprouting and the desert bursts into bloom.

The abal plant is sometimes called the "firebush" because its roots make good firewood.

Many different types of bushes and trees grow in the Arabian Desert. The ghaf tree has very long roots which can reach 30 metres down to suck up water from deep underground. It can also soak up moisture from dew and mist carried in from the Arabian Sea. Ghaf trees are sometimes planted on sand dunes. Their roots bind the sand together and stop the dunes from moving, and the desert spreading.

ghaf tree

acacia tree

thorns

Acacia trees have bright yellow
flowers and green leaves. They have
sharp thorns at the base of their leaves to warn off
hungry animals. Like ghaf trees, acacias have very long
roots for reaching water. Their seed pods are used as food
for animals.

Did you know?

The toothbrush tree is a small
tree with a crooked trunk.
It gets its nickname because
local people use its twigs to
brush their teeth. The plant
contains natural chemicals that
kill germs and keep teeth clean.

An oasis is a place in the desert where underground water comes to the surface. It creates a **fertile** patch of land where people can grow crops, such as date palms. These are probably the most famous plants in the desert, and the most useful.

Date palms can grow more than 20 metres tall. They have long spiky trunks and **frond**-like leaves. Desert people use every part of the tree – fruit (dates) for eating, leaves for making baskets and thatching roofs, wood for building, and fibres for making rope. Even the date stones can be used as food for cattle.

oasis in the Arabian Desert

Dates have been grown and eaten for thousands of years in Arabia. Desert people relied on them to survive. On long journeys, they lived on supplies of camel milk and dates packed in palm leaves to make them last. Dates are still eaten at festival times, and offered to guests.

date palm

Animal survival

Many animals also thrive in the desert, even though food and water are hard to find. Staying cool is another challenge. Some animals survive the heat by only coming out at night. During the day, they rest in the shade of rocks or plants, or hide away in underground burrows.

Jerboas are small rodents, with big ears, long back legs and long tails. They rest in burrows during the day; then come out at night to find food. They mainly eat desert plants. They use their big ears for listening out for predators, and their long back legs for hopping away.

jerboa

24

Rüppell's foxes are well suited to desert life. They have large ears that help them to lose heat from their bodies, and to listen out for prey. Their feet have furry pads to protect them from the heat of the sand.

Rüppell's fox

The Arabian oryx is a beautiful antelope that lives in the desert. About 50 years ago, so many oryxes had been killed by hunters that they became **extinct**. The only oryxes left were found in zoos. Some zoos were able to breed oryxes and put them back into the wild.

Arabian oryx

The oryx has many features to help it survive. Its white coat reflects the sun's rays and keeps it cool. Its wide hooves spread out across the soft sand and stop it sinking as it walks.

It's very hot during the day, so oryxes are active in the early morning and late evening when it's cooler. In the daytime, they dig **scrapes** in the ground where they can lie down in the cooler sand, out of the fierce desert wind.

Did you know?

Oryxes can sniff out rain from far away. Then they set off in search of plants that have sprouted in the rain, often walking long distances to find food.

Desert insects include flies, mosquitoes, ants, locusts and **dung** beetles. Using their back feet, dung beetles roll animal dung into balls. Then they roll the balls to a safe place and lay their eggs in them. When the beetle grubs hatch, they have a ready supply of dung to feed on.

Did you know?

Desert white butterflies can survive in the driest parts of the desert by speeding up their life cycle. They spend years as **pupae**, waiting for the rain to come and plants to grow. Then, they quickly turn into adults which feed on the plants. The adults mate and lay their eggs which hatch and become pupae.

desert white butterfly

Other desert creepy-crawlies include spiders and scorpions. The Arabian fat-tailed scorpion has a thick, strong tail, with a sting at the end. Its sting injects deadly **venom** into its prey of insects and spiders. The scorpion is about ten centimetres long. It hides in a burrow or under a rock during the day, and comes out at night to hunt for food.

Arabian fat-tailed scorpion

To warn off enemies, the saw-scaled viper rubs its scales together to make a sawing or rasping sound. Experts think that this wastes less water than hissing a warning. This deadly poisonous desert snake moves by flipping its body sideways across the sand. Because its body only touches the sand for a few seconds, it doesn't overheat.

saw-scaled viper

The sandfish is a small lizard with a body designed for "swimming" through the sand. It has a **streamlined** shape, with smooth skin and a long snout. It moves its legs back and forth as if it's swimming front crawl. Its ears are small but sharp enough for locating insects underneath the sand.

sandfish

Spiny-tailed lizards live in deep burrows where they shelter from danger and the heat. These large lizards get their name from their spiny tails. The tails are prized by the Bedouin people who hunt the lizards for their meat and skin.

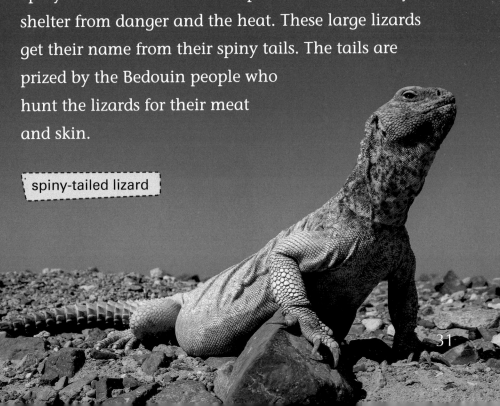

spiny-tailed lizard

Sandgrouse are small birds that lay their eggs in nests on the ground. When the chicks hatch, the male flies off to a water hole, which is often many kilometres away. The feathers on his belly are specially designed for soaking up water. Back at the nest, the chicks suck the water from the feathers.

A fierce hunter, the saker falcon flies fast above the ground, searching for rodents and other animals. Then it grasps its prey with the sharp, curved talons on its feet, and tears it apart with its strong, hooked beak. The Bedouin have caught falcons for centuries and trained them for hunting.

Sandgrouse are pigeon-sized birds with sandy-brown feathers for camouflage.

saker falcon

Did you know?

The Arabian Desert is an important stopping-off place for millions of birds, such as bee-eaters, larks and swifts. Each year, these birds **migrate** across the desert and along the coast on their way between Europe, Asia and Africa.

Desert people

People have lived in the Arabian Desert for thousands of years. They've learnt how to survive in the hostile climate, and how to find enough to eat and drink.

The Bedouin people are an Arab people whose name means "desert dweller". They traditionally live as nomads, moving from place to place, in search of food and water for their herds of camels, sheep and goats. To suit their nomadic lifestyle, the Bedouin live in tents which are quick to put up and take down.

Bedouin tents are woven from goats' hair or sheep's wool, and are designed to stay cool in the day and warm at night.

Did you know?

The Bedouin wear clothes that are adapted to desert life. Long, loose robes protect them from the sun but allow cool air to circulate. Headdresses stop sunburn and also keep out dust and sand.

Camels play a very important part in Bedouin life. Without them, the Bedouin wouldn't have been able to survive in the desert. The Bedouin drink camel milk, use their wool for ropes, their skin for leather and their dung for fires. Camels are also used for transport. They are treated as part of the family, and even have songs sung to them to keep them happy and strong.

camel racing in the desert

Did you know?

Camels are a sign of wealth in Bedouin society. The more camels you have, the more important you are. They are also given as part of a **dowry** at a Bedouin wedding.

Camels are perfectly adapted to desert life. They can go for days without water, and survive for weeks without food, using fat stored in their humps. Their long legs hold their bodies off the hot ground as they walk, and their wide, flat feet spread their weight over the soft sand. Two rows of thick eyelashes keep the sand out of their eyes.

thick eyelashes

hump

The one-humped camels found in the Arabian Desert are called dromedaries.

long legs

wide feet

The Bedouin are Muslims, who follow the religion of Islam which began in Arabia around 1,400 years ago. Muslims believe in Allah (God) and the Prophet Muhammad who taught people how to live and worship Allah. Like all Muslims, the Bedouin pray five times a day, facing Makkah, the holy city of Islam in Saudi Arabia.

a Bedouin praying

Bedouin resting in the shade

The Bedouin are famous for their hospitality.
In the desert, where there are very few travellers, guests
are always made welcome. A rug is spread out on
the floor of the tent, and guests are served tea or coffee.
Afterwards, there may be a feast with music and poetry.

Poetry is very popular with the Bedouin and is a way
of passing down their history. The poems are learnt by
heart, and then recited from memory. They tell stories of
great deeds and adventures from the past, and express
feelings of love, sadness and anger.

39

Today, many Bedouin have given up their nomadic life and settled in villages around oases, or in desert cities. Modern cities are growing up all over the Arabian Desert, paid for with the profits from the booming oil business. The cities are home to millions of people.

Israel

Kuwait City

Buraydah   Al Dammam

Medina   Doha   Dubai

Jeddah   Abu Dhabi

Riyadh

Al Ta'if

Abha

modern cities are growing up all around the Arabian Desert

desert village around an oasis

Dubai is a desert city in the United Arab Emirates (UAE), located on the coast of the Arabian Gulf. It's one of the wealthiest cities in the world, and a major transport hub. It's famous for its amazing architecture, especially its skyscrapers and other high-rise buildings.

Each year, millions of tourists visit Dubai to enjoy the warm weather, relax on the beaches and go shopping. The Dubai Mall is the biggest shopping centre in the world. It has more than 1,200 shops, a luxury hotel, cinemas, restaurants, an aquarium, an ice rink and an indoor theme park.

At 829.8 metres, the Burj Khalifa in Dubai is the world's tallest building.

For centuries, camels were the main form of transport in the desert because they could carry heavy loads over long distances. Arab traders carried gold, spices, ivory and precious stones across the desert on the back of camels, between Arabia, Europe and Asia.

Camels are still used but, since the discovery of oil, there have been great changes in desert transport. Trucks, cars and aircraft have made travel much quicker and easier. Huge, modern highways now link the main desert cities. Highway 40 in Saudi Arabia runs for around 1,400 kilometres across the desert.

highways in the desert

42

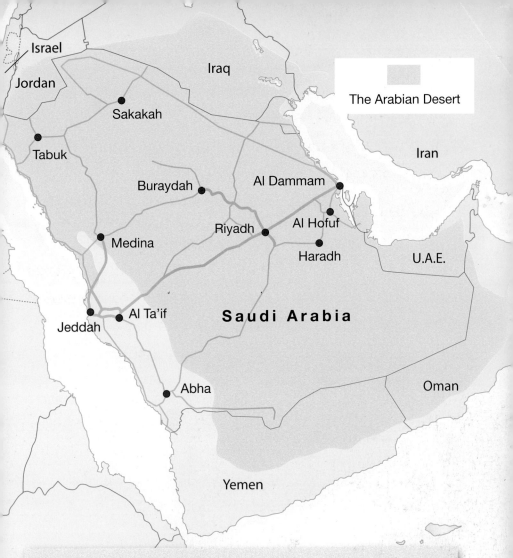

Israel

Iraq

Jordan

Sakakah

The Arabian Desert

Tabuk

Iran

Buraydah

Al Dammam

Medina

Riyadh

Al Hofuf

Haradh

U.A.E.

Al Ta'if

S a u d i   A r a b i a

Jeddah

Abha

Oman

Yemen

Did you know?

Building a road across the Arabian Desert isn't an easy task. The road surface has to be carefully chosen so that it doesn't melt in the heat. There are also many mountains in the way. Cuttings have to be blasted through the rock to allow a road to run through.

Riches of the desert

Large parts of the Arabian Desert may look bare and dry, but some very valuable resources are buried beneath the sand. Vast **reservoirs** of water, called aquifers, lie deep underground. Thousands of wells have been drilled down into them to get water for cities, farming and industry.

This well taps into an aquifer that's thousands of years old.

The sea is another major source of water. At a **desalination** plant, salt is removed from sea water to make it suitable for drinking. About two thirds of the drinking water in Saudi Arabia is produced in this way. The largest desalination plant produces around one million cubic metres of water a day – enough to fill 400 Olympic-sized swimming pools.

A new desalination plant is being built in Saudi Arabia. It'll be powered by solar energy to make use of another desert resource – the sun. It's due to open in 2017.

a desalination plant

Huge quantities of oil and gas have
been found in rocks deep under
the Arabian Desert. Today, the desert
produces around a fifth of the world's oil,
making countries such as Saudi Arabia,
the UAE and Kuwait very rich indeed.
These countries earn billions of pounds by
selling oil and gas around the world.

To extract the oil from the desert, **geologists**
first study the rocks to see where the oil is
trapped under the ground. Then oil workers
drill down thousands of metres to reach
the oil. It's pumped out of the ground and
carried across the desert in giant pipelines
to oil **refineries** along
the coast.

Oil was first discovered in
the Arabian Desert in the 1930s.

Pipelines carry oil and gas across the desert.

Did you know?

Although there are around 100 major oil and gas fields in Saudi Arabia, half of the country's oil comes from eight gigantic fields. The biggest is the Ghawar Field which produces more than five million barrels of oil a day.

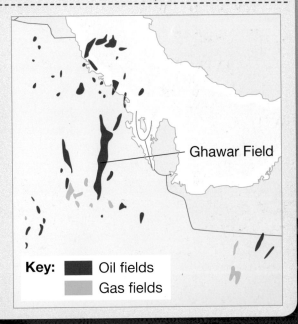

Ghawar Field

Key:
■ Oil fields
■ Gas fields

Using the desert's resources has allowed Saudi Arabia and its neighbouring countries to grow fast and become very rich. But it can also cause problems for the fragile desert environment and its wildlife.

About 40 years ago, there was enough underground water in the desert aquifers to fill Lake Erie in the USA, one of the world's biggest lakes. But so much water has been used for farms and growing cities that the supply is shrinking fast. With no rain to refill the aquifers, water shortages could be a major problem in the future.

With so little rain, farmers must bring water to the desert so that crops can grow.

sewage being pumped into the Arabian Gulf

Oil spills, leaking pipelines and waste water from oil refineries can also be devastating. If oil is spilt along the coast, it **pollutes** the water and can kill ocean animals and birds. The oil clogs up birds' feathers so that they can't keep warm or stay afloat. Other animals are poisoned if they swallow any oil.

Changing desert

Life in the Arabian Desert is changing fast. In some places, new cities are being built. In other places, the desert is spreading.

The way deserts spread is called desertification. This can happen naturally because of climate change, but people are also adding to the problem. They are overusing the land at the edges of the desert for farming and grazing their animals. The land quickly turns to dust and is easily blown away. Huge areas of land around the Arabian Desert are in danger. Some countries, such as Qatar, have now set up tree-planting schemes to try to hold the desert back.

Rows of bushes have been planted to stop the sand covering the road in the UAE.

Desertification is just one of the challenges facing the desert in the future. With the growing number of cities, there's more pressure on water, and precious oil supplies will not last for ever. Some cities are now experimenting with using renewable energy to provide them with power. Life for desert people is changing, too, with traditional ways disappearing. For now, though, it's still possible to see Bedouin camels side-by-side with the latest high-tech transport – old and new!

When it's finished in 2020, King Abdullah Economic City (KAEC) in Saudi Arabia will be bigger than Washington DC, USA, and home to around two million people.

Glossary

desalination	process of removing salt from sea water
dowry	money and other goods that a bride presents to a groom
dung	animal droppings
extinct	died out for ever
fertile	able to produce plant life
frond	a long leaf with many small pieces, like a fern
geologists	scientists who study the Earth and rocks
lava	rock that comes out of a volcano and hardens in the air
migrate	when an animal makes a long journey to breed and feed
parallel	lines that never touch but keep an equal distance apart
peninsula	narrow piece of land jutting out into the sea from the mainland
plateaux	wide, flat areas of high land
pollutes	makes dirty
pupae	stage of an insect's life cycle between larvae (grubs) and adults
refineries	factories where oil is processed, ready for sale
reservoirs	natural or artificial lakes used for collecting and storing water
scrapes	shallow holes
streamlined	smooth body shape that cuts easily through air, water or sand
venom	poison made by animals

Index

animals   15, 18, 21,
   24–33, 49, 50

Bedouin   13, 31–32,
   34–36, 38–40, 51

camels   13, 23, 34, 36–37,
   42, 51

cities   40–42, 44, 48,
   50–51

cliffs   8

Dubai   41

erg   5

mountains   8, 43

oases   22, 40

oil   40, 42, 46–47, 49, 51

plants   18–24, 27–28

rain   2, 8, 14, 19, 27–28,
   48

Rub al Khali   4–7

sand   2, 4–5, 8, 10–11,
   16–17, 20, 25, 27, 30–31,
   35, 37, 44, 50

sand dunes   5, 6, 16, 18,
   20

Saudi Arabia   2, 16, 38,
   42, 45–48, 51

temperature   12

wadis   8, 14

water   4, 8, 11, 13, 18–22,
   24, 30, 32, 34, 37, 44–45,
   48–49, 51

wind   4, 6–7, 10, 16–17, 27

Arabian Desert quiz

1 Where's the Arabian Desert?
   a) in Antarctica
   b) in Africa
   c) in the Middle East

2 What's an erg?
   a) a sand dune
   b) a type of rock
   c) a sea of sand

3 What shape are barchan dunes?
   a) crescent-shaped
   b) sword-shaped
   c) camel-shaped

4 Weather in the day time is usually ...
   a) cold and icy
   b) hot and dry
   c) warm and wet

5 What's a "brown roller"?
   a) a type of camel
   b) a sand and dust storm
   c) a desert vehicle

6 How do jerboas stay cool?
  a) come out at night
  b) spit on their fur
  c) rest underground

7 Where do dung beetles lay their eggs?
  a) in plant stems
  b) in balls of animal droppings
  c) in sand dunes

8 Where do the Bedouin traditionally live?
  a) in apartment blocks
  b) in wooden huts
  c) in tents made from goats' and sheep's wool

9 What's an aquifer?
  a) an underground pool of water
  b) a type of food made from dates
  c) a robe worn by the Bedouin

10 How much of the world's oil comes from the Arabian Desert?
  a) all of it
  b) about a fifth of it
  c) about half of it

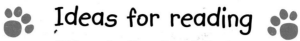

Ideas for reading

Written by Clare Dowdall, PhD
Lecturer and Primary Literacy Consultant

Reading objectives:
- ask questions to improve their understanding
- summarise the main ideas drawn from more than one paragraph, identifying key details that support the main ideas
- retrieve, record and present information from non-fiction

Spoken language objectives:
- give well-structured descriptions, explanations and narratives for different purposes

Curriculum links: Geography – place knowledge; Science – living things and their habitats

Resources: map of the world, ICT, pens and paper

Build a context for reading

- Explain that you will be reading about the Arabian Desert. Locate the Arabian Desert on a map of the world.
- Ask children to close their eyes and imagine they are in the Arabian Desert. What can they hear, smell and feel? Discuss whether children would like to visit the Arabian Desert for a holiday.
- Look at the cover and read the blurb together. Gather suggestions about the types of plants, animals and people who might live in the Arabian Desert.

Understand and apply reading strategies

- Read pp2–3 together. Look closely at the map on p3. Ask children to share any knowledge that they have about the Arabian Peninsula, based on knowledge of the place names featured.